pasta

pasta

SILVANA FRANCO

PHOTOGRAPHY BY **WILLIAM LINGWOOD**

RYLAND
PETERS
& SMALL

LONDON NEW YORK

Author's acknowledgements

First thanks, as always, to Jenny and Angela at Fork for being ace, to Sharon for her ever-cheerful assistance, to the talented William Lingwood, and to Sally Somers at Ryland Peters & Small for being such a pleasure to work with. Finally, love and thanks to the family Franco and my sweetheart, the lovely Roberto.

The author and publisher would like to thank the following stores for the loan of props that appear in this book: Aria (020 7704 1999), Divertimenti (020 7581 8065), Purves & Purves (020 7580 8223) and Skandium (020 7935 2077).

Notes

All spoon measurements are level unless otherwise specified. Fresh herbs are used in this book unless otherwise stated. If using dried herbs, halve the quantity given.
Uncooked or partly cooked eggs should not be served to the very old or frail, the very young or to pregnant women.
Ovens should be preheated to the specified temperature. Recipes in this book were tested with a fan-assisted oven. If using a regular oven, increase the cooking times according to the manufacturer's instructions.

First published in Great Britain in 2002
by Ryland Peters & Small
Kirkman House, 12–14 Whitfield Street, London W1T 2RP
www.rylandpeters.com
10 9 8 7 6 5 4 3 2

Text, design and photographs © Ryland Peters & Small 2002

ISBN 1 84172 260 X

A catalogue record for this book is available from the British Library.

Printed and bound in China

Designer
Emilie Ekström

Commissioning Editor
Elsa Petersen-Schepelern

Editor
Sally Somers

Production
Patricia Harrington

Art Director
Gabriella Le Grazie

Publishing Director
Alison Starling

Food Stylist
Silvana Franco

Stylist
Helen Trent

Photographer's Assistant
Emma Bentham-Wood

CONTENTS

FAST FOOD AT ITS BEST...

For those of us who lead busy lives but still want to eat healthy and fresh food, pasta is often the first choice – it's one of the few dishes that can be ready to eat within half an hour of getting home. Pasta makes such ideal everyday food, not only because it's so quick and easy, but also because it can be incredibly varied. In this book you'll find a fantastic range of homemade sauces, all using readily available ingredients. Pasta goes with almost everything; meat, seafood, vegetables, cheese – the list is endless. Many of the sauces in this book can be made in the time it takes to boil the pasta, while others can be prepared ahead of time and reheated, making life even easier.

I have included dried pasta weights in the recipes, because I would only recommend fresh pasta when you want ready-stuffed shapes. A simple sauce, such as Tomato with Double Basil on page 12, can go really well with fresh shapes, but in general I would advise you to buy good-quality dried pasta, made with 100 per cent durum wheat. It cooks to a firm and springy bite (known in Italian as *al dente*), comes in a huge range of shapes and sizes, and is very convenient to buy and store. If you have a little more time and energy to spare, then making and stuffing your own pasta is surprisingly easy and satisfying – it will never fail to impress!

PARMESAN – YES OR NO?

Generally, yes. Have a small block of Parmesan with a fine grater and pass them around the table so everyone can grate their own. The only time Parmesan should not be offered is if the sauce is fish or seafood. It just doesn't go, and you would certainly never see it on an Italian table. That said, if the seafood or fish sauce is creamy, for some reason a grating of Parmesan can be more than welcome. Pecorino, also a hard cheese but made from sheeps' milk, has a tangy flavour and can be a good alternative to Parmesan. It is now quite widely available in good cheese shops and supermarkets.

DRIED PASTA TYPES

There's a huge selection of dried pasta shapes, sizes and lengths available. These can be divided into basic categories of strands, ribbons, tubes and shapes. Your choice will largely depend on the type of sauce you are serving with it. Strands (such as spaghetti) and ribbons (such as fettuccine) are ideal paired with fine and oil-based sauces, which coat the strands evenly. Tubes (such as penne) or shapes (such as conchiglie) go well with chunky or meaty sauces, as they nestle together in the bowl and catch the sauce inside their shapes. But these are just guidelines, not a set of rules – there will always be exceptions, so you should choose pairings that you like or that simply suit your mood.

STRANDS AND RIBBONS

Long pasta, known as 'pasta lunga', comes either as long strands (hollow or solid) or as flat ribbons, called 'fettucce'.

Strands: spaghetti (right), spaghettini, bucatini – which are hollow.

Ribbons: tagliatelle (right), linguine, tagliolini, fettuccine, pappardelle.

TUBES AND SHAPES

Tubes and shapes are either plain or ridged – 'rigati'. The ridges help the sauce cling to the pasta.

Tubes: penne (right), chifferi, rigatoni, macaroni or maccheroni.

Shapes: fusilli (right), conchiglie (right), farfalle, orecchiette, gemelli.

PASTA FOR SOUPS

Very small shapes are ideal for soups, as they look very pretty and delicate and don't dominate the soup.

Soup pasta: anellini (right) fedelini, stelline, alfabetini, ditali.

PASTA FOR BAKING

Lasagne are flat sheets of pasta, layered with sauce in baked dishes. Cannelloni (right) are large tubes for stuffing and baking.

FLAVOURED PASTA

Pasta flavoured and coloured with spinach, tomato or squid ink are the most common, although beetroot, basil and saffron flavour are also available.

Cannelloni

Conchiglie

Tagliatelle

COOKING DRIED PASTA

- Allow 75–125 g dried pasta per person, depending on how substantial the sauce is and, of course, on appetites.
- Cook pasta in a large saucepan with plenty of salted, boiling water, at least 4 litres per 500 g pasta. Don't skimp on the salt, or the pasta will taste bland – add it to the water just before you add the pasta.
- Add the pasta to the boiling water all at once.
- Keep the water boiling and cook with the lid off. Stir with a wooden fork to stop it sticking, but don't add oil to the water: it's a waste of oil.
- Don't overdrain and never rinse cooked pasta – the coat of starch helps the sauce cling. Reserve a cup of pasta cooking water before you drain, then add it to the sauce if it seems dry.
- Cook until *al dente*, literally 'to the tooth', testing often by removing a strand or shape and tasting it. *Al dente* pasta is springy – when it is overcooked it is flabby and when undercooked has a chalky centre.
- Don't delay – pasta gets cold quickly. Return drained pasta to the warm pan or to a warmed serving bowl, add the sauce, toss with a fork and spoon, then serve.

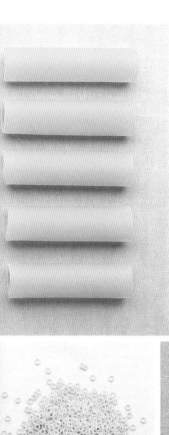

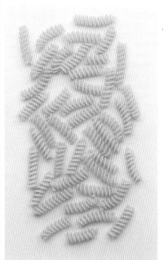

Fusilli

Spaghetti

Anellini

Penne

FRESH PASTA DOUGH

There's something really satisfying about making pasta at home. I always use a food processor and pasta machine, but you can easily make and roll the dough by hand. Try to find Italian tipo OO flour but, if unavailable, opt for a strong bread flour. Eggs add richness and colour and make the dough softer and easier to work.

300 g pasta flour, such as tipo 00, plus extra for kneading and rolling

a pinch of salt

3 small eggs

Makes 500 g

Put the flour and salt into a food processor, then add the eggs. Process in short bursts until the mixture forms sticky crumbs. Alternatively, to make the dough by hand, sieve the flour into a bowl, sprinkle with salt and make a well in the middle. Add the eggs to the well and, using your hands, gradually work the flour into the eggs, using circular motions.

Transfer the mixture to a lightly floured surface and bring together with your hands to form a soft dough.

Knead the dough for about 5 minutes, until it feels smooth, then wrap in clingfilm and chill for about 30 minutes, but for no more than 1 hour. Chilling is essential, and will make the dough easier to roll and less likely to tear.

Divide the pasta into 4 pieces, and roll each piece through a pasta machine, going down a setting each time and dusting with flour when necessary, up to and including the thinnest setting. If you don't have a pasta machine, roll out the dough with a rolling pin on a lightly floured surface to about 2–3 mm.

Note If the pasta is to be filled, use each sheet immediately after rolling, or the pasta will start to dry out and crack when handled. If you are making plain ribbons, strands or shapes, leave the sheets of dough to dry on a clean tea towel for about 30 minutes before cutting. They can be left to dry out for up to 2 days before cooking.

classic sauces

TOMATO WITH DOUBLE BASIL

In summer, make this with fragrant, ripe tomatoes –
otherwise, use canned Italian plum tomatoes. The basil is
added in two stages; first for depth of flavour, then at the
end for a burst of fresh fragrance – double basil.

3 tablespoons olive oil

**2 garlic cloves,
finely chopped**

1 shallot, finely chopped

25 g basil leaves

**500 g ripe tomatoes,
coarsely chopped,
or 400 g canned plum
tomatoes**

a pinch of sugar

**350 g dried pasta, such as
spaghetti or linguine**

**salt and freshly
ground black pepper**

**freshly grated Parmesan
cheese, to serve**

Serves 4

Heat the oil in a saucepan and add
the garlic, shallot and half the basil.
Cook for 3–4 minutes until the
shallot is golden.

Add the tomatoes and cook, stirring,
for 10 minutes, until thickened and
pulpy. Add the sugar, 100 ml water
and salt and pepper to taste.

Bring to the boil, cover and simmer
very gently for 1 hour until dark red
and thickened, with droplets of oil
on the surface.

Bring a large saucepan of water to
the boil. Add a good pinch of salt,
then the pasta, and cook until *al
dente*, or according to the timings
on the packet.

Drain and return the pasta to the
warm pan. Tear the remaining basil
into the tomato sauce and add the
sauce to the pasta. Toss to mix, then
serve topped with Parmesan.

CRISPY CRUMBS

These make a great addition to any tomato-sauce-based pasta. Heat a couple of tablespoons of olive oil in a frying pan and add a good handful or two of fresh white breadcrumbs. Cook over a high heat, stirring until golden brown. The smaller crumbs will go to the bottom of the pan and char a little, but that's good. Serve straight from the pan, sprinkled on top of the pasta, while the crumbs are still hot and sizzling.

CLASSIC BASIL PESTO

Toast the pine nuts in a dry frying pan until golden for a variation of this vibrant basil sauce.

50 g basil leaves

2 tablespoons pine nuts

2 garlic cloves

2 tablespoons olive oil

50 g butter, softened

50 g freshly grated Parmesan cheese

350 g dried pasta, such as spaghetti

freshly ground black pepper

Serves 4

Put the basil, pine nuts and garlic into a food processor and process until finely chopped. Add the oil, butter, Parmesan and freshly ground black pepper to taste. Process briefly until blended.

Bring a large saucepan of water to the boil. Add a good pinch of salt, then the pasta, and cook until *al dente*, or according to the timings on the packet.

Drain and return the pasta to the warm pan. Add the pesto and toss to mix. Serve topped with extra Parmesan.

Note Pesto can be refrigerated for up to 4 days. Transfer to a lidded jar or cover with clingfilm.

BOLOGNESE SAUCE

Like many classic, handed-down recipes, there are countless versions of Bolognese Sauce. Some Italian chefs add sweetbreads, chicken livers and veal, but here I've opted for a mixture of beef mince and Parma ham. I find that it really benefits from being chilled overnight, so it's ideal for making the day before and gently reheating.

10 g dried porcini mushrooms, rinsed

Put the porcini into a bowl, cover with boiling water and set aside for 20 minutes until softened.

1 tablespoon olive oil

1 onion, finely chopped

500 g beef mince

Heat the oil in a large saucepan, add the onion and cook for 2 minutes. Add the beef mince and Parma ham and cook for 3–4 minutes, stirring, until evenly browned.

50 g Parma ham, coarsely chopped

100 ml Marsala or sherry

700 ml tomato passata

Drain the porcini and discard the soaking water. Chop the porcini, then add to the pan with the Marsala and passata. Cover and simmer for 1 hour, stirring occasionally, until rich and dark. Add salt and pepper to taste.

300 g dried pasta, such as spaghetti or linguine

salt and freshly ground black pepper

Meanwhile, bring a large saucepan of water to the boil. Add a good pinch of salt, then the pasta, and cook until *al dente*, or according to the timings on the packet.

fresh shavings of Parmesan cheese, to serve

Serves 4

Drain the pasta and divide between 4 serving plates or bowls. Top with Bolognese Sauce and Parmesan shavings, then serve.

CREAMY VODKA SAUCE

Vodka and tomato are a classic combination – think of Bloody Mary – and here they make a creamy, mild sauce that is fast becoming a regular on restaurant menus. If you haven't got chilli vodka, add a small, finely chopped chilli at the same time as the garlic and use ordinary vodka.

CARBONARA

Brilliant for a quick after-work supper – ready to eat in the time it takes the pasta to cook. It's traditionally served with spaghetti, but any long or ribbon shape, such as tagliatelle or linguine, will be fine.

200 g dried pasta, such as spaghetti or linguine

1 tablespoon butter

1 shallot, finely chopped

2 garlic cloves, finely chopped

6 slices smoked streaky bacon, chopped

2 eggs

150 ml single cream

2 tablespoons freshly grated Parmesan cheese, plus extra to serve

salt and freshly ground black pepper

Serves 2

Bring a large saucepan of water to the boil. Add a good pinch of salt, then the pasta, and cook until *al dente*, or according to the timings on the packet.

Meanwhile, heat the butter in a small frying pan, add the shallot, garlic and bacon and cook for 5 minutes until golden. Put the eggs, cream and Parmesan into a bowl and beat, adding salt and pepper to taste.

Drain the pasta and return it to the warm pan. Remove from the heat and add the shallot mixture. Add the egg mixture and toss well to coat. Divide between 2 serving bowls, sprinkle with Parmesan and black pepper, then serve.

ALFREDO VARIATION

Alfredo sauce is very similar to Carbonara but even simpler. Toss hot cooked pasta (traditionally linguine) with double cream, butter and grated Parmesan, sprinkle with black pepper and serve.

250 g dried pasta, such as fusilli or fusilli bucati

1 tablespoon butter

2 plum tomatoes, coarsely chopped

1 garlic clove, finely chopped

4 tablespoons chilli vodka

150 ml double cream

salt and freshly ground black pepper

to serve
a few chives, halved

freshly grated Parmesan cheese

Serves 2

Bring a large saucepan of water to the boil. Add a good pinch of salt, then the pasta, and cook until *al dente*, or according to the timings on the packet.

Meanwhile, heat the butter in a small saucepan, add the tomatoes and garlic and cook for 3 minutes. Add the vodka and boil rapidly for 2 minutes. Reduce the heat and simmer for 2–3 minutes, then stir in the cream and simmer gently for a further 5 minutes. Add salt and pepper to taste.

Drain the pasta and return it to the warm pan. Add the creamy sauce to the pasta and mix well. Transfer to 2 serving bowls and top with chives. Sprinkle with plenty of Parmesan and black pepper and serve.

Puttanesca was famously named in honour of the ladies of the night, although no-one seems quite sure why. I like to think it's because the sauce has a wild and fiery character. This robust dish is perfectly matched by a full-bodied red wine.

PUTTANESCA

2 tablespoons olive oil

1 onion, finely chopped

2 garlic cloves, finely chopped

4 anchovy fillets in oil, drained and coarsely chopped

2 red chillies, finely chopped

4 ripe tomatoes, coarsely chopped

1 tablespoon salted capers, rinsed well and coarsely chopped

100 ml red wine

350 g dried pasta, such as gemelli or penne

75 g small black olives

2 tablespoons chopped fresh flat leaf parsley

freshly ground black pepper

freshly grated Parmesan cheese, to serve

Serves 4

Heat the oil in a saucepan, then add the onion, garlic, anchovies and chillies. Cook over medium heat for 4–5 minutes until softened and golden. Add the tomatoes and cook for 3–4 minutes, stirring occasionally, until softened.

Add the capers, wine and black pepper to taste, then cover and simmer for 20 minutes.

Meanwhile, bring a large saucepan of water to the boil. Add a good pinch of salt, then the pasta, and cook until *al dente*, or according to the timings on the packet.

Drain well and return the pasta to the warm pan. Add the tomato sauce, olives and parsley and toss to mix. Divide between 4 bowls and serve topped with grated Parmesan.

VONGOLE

The clams are the stars of this dish, but it's crucial that the sauce is smooth. If you only have canned tomatoes, purée them with a hand blender or press them through a sieve before using. Delicious as this is, it's not an elegant meal to eat, so be prepared: tie your napkin firmly round your neck and use your fingers to pick the clams from their shells.

2 tablespoons olive oil

2 garlic cloves, finely chopped

a sprig of rosemary

500 ml tomato passata

½ teaspoon sugar

300 g dried pasta, such as spaghetti or linguine

1 kg fresh baby clams or cockles in shells

2 tablespoons chopped fresh flat leaf parsley

salt and freshly ground black pepper

Serves 4

Heat the oil in a saucepan, add the garlic and rosemary and cook for 2 minutes. Add the passata and sugar, with salt and pepper to taste. Bring to the boil, cover and simmer for 30 minutes, then remove and discard the sprig of rosemary.

Meanwhile, bring a large saucepan of water to the boil. Add a good pinch of salt, then the pasta, and cook until *al dente,* or according to the timings on the packet.

While the pasta is cooking, put the clams and 2 tablespoons water into another large saucepan. Cover and cook over medium heat for 4–5 minutes, shaking the pan occasionally until all the shells have opened, and discarding any that remain closed.

Strain the clam cooking juices through a sieve into the tomato pan, to remove grit. When the clams are cool enough to handle, shell half of them and discard the empty shells. Add the shelled and unshelled clams to the tomato sauce and simmer for 3–4 minutes.

Drain the pasta and return it to the warm pan. Add the clams and parsley and toss to mix. Divide between 4 bowls and serve.

SEAFOOD SPAGHETTINI

Vary the seafood depending on what's available and best on the day, but always include clams or mussels – for their flavour as well as their beautiful shells.

300 g dried pasta, such as spaghettini

4–5 tablespoons olive oil

1 garlic clove, finely chopped

300 g mixed seafood, such as squid, cut into rings, shelled prawns and scallops, halved crossways

500 g fresh mussels or clams in shells, scrubbed

2 tablespoons chopped fresh flat leaf parsley

sea salt and freshly ground black pepper

Serves 4

Bring a large saucepan of water to the boil. Add a good pinch of salt, then the pasta, and cook until *al dente,* or according to the timings on the packet.

Meanwhile, heat half the oil in a large sauté pan or saucepan. Add the mixed seafood and cook for 3–4 minutes, stirring constantly until just cooked. Transfer to a large bowl and set aside.

Add the mussels or clams to the seafood pan, cover with a lid and cook for 5 minutes until all the shells have opened, discarding any that remain closed.

Drain the pasta well and return it to the warm pan. Add the mussels or clams, seafood, remaining olive oil and parsley. Add salt and pepper to taste, toss gently to mix, then serve.

meat and seafood

ITALIAN STEAK SAUCE

The traditional way to eat this would be to serve the sauce with the pasta and to follow with the steak, a selection of salads and some crusty bread. I like to serve it with the steak cut into slices and mixed with the pasta and sauce.

1 tablespoon chopped fresh rosemary

2 tablespoons chopped fresh flat leaf parsley, plus extra to serve

2 garlic cloves, crushed

4 semi-dried sunblush tomatoes, or sun-dried tomatoes

2 teaspoons salted capers, rinsed well

8 minute steaks, 50 g each

1 tablespoon olive oil

800 g canned plum tomatoes

300 g dried pasta, such as conchiglie or rigatoni

salt and freshly ground black pepper

Serves 4

Put the rosemary, parsley, garlic, semi-dried or sun-dried tomatoes and capers into a food processor and process until finely chopped.

Put the steaks flat onto a work surface and sprinkle lightly with salt and freshly ground black pepper. Spread the herb mixture evenly over each steak and roll up tightly, tying string around the middle to secure.

Heat the olive oil until very hot in a large sauté pan, add the rolled steaks and cook for 2–3 minutes until browned all over. Add the canned tomatoes and salt and pepper to taste. Cover and simmer for 1 hour, then remove the lid and cook for a further 20 minutes until the meat is tender and sauce is thickened and pulpy.

Meanwhile, bring a large saucepan of water to the boil. Add a good pinch of salt, then the pasta, and cook until *al dente*, or according to the timings on the packet.

Transfer the steaks from the sauce to a chopping board. Remove and discard the string, then cut each steak crossways into chunky slices.

Drain the pasta and return it to the warm pan. Add the sauce and steak to the pasta and toss to mix. Divide between 4 bowls or plates, top with parsley and serve.

PANCETTA AND CHICKEN MEATBALLS

Meatballs are a time-honoured accompaniment to pasta. These delicious little mouthfuls are made with chicken, bacon and herbs, so are somewhat lighter than the traditional all-meat versions.

500 g chicken mince

50 g thinly sliced pancetta, coarsely chopped

6 spring onions, finely chopped

4 garlic cloves, finely chopped

2 red chillies, deseeded and finely chopped

4 tablespoons freshly grated Parmesan cheese, plus extra to serve

1 tablespoon fresh thyme leaves

1 tablespoon olive oil

200 ml red wine

800 g canned plum tomatoes

a pinch of sugar

300 g dried pasta, such as gnocchi or conchiglie

salt and freshly ground black pepper

Serves 4

Put the chicken mince, pancetta, spring onion, garlic, chilli, Parmesan and thyme into a bowl. Add plenty of salt and pepper and mix well. Using your hands, shape into 24 small, firm balls.

Heat the oil in a large saucepan, add the meatballs and cook for about 5 minutes, turning them frequently until browned all over. Add the wine and simmer vigorously for 1–2 minutes.

Add the tomatoes, breaking them up with a wooden spoon. Stir in the sugar, and add salt and pepper to taste. Bring to the boil, then simmer very gently, uncovered, for 30 minutes until the sauce is rich and thickened.

Meanwhile, bring a large saucepan of water to the boil. Add a good pinch of salt, then the pasta, and cook until *al dente,* or according to the timings on the packet.

Drain the pasta well and return it to the warm pan. Add the meatballs and sauce to the pasta, toss well to mix, then divide between 4 bowls. Serve topped with extra Parmesan.

The Parma ham crisps up beautifully in a non-stick frying pan – other cured hams can also be used, such as serrano, San Daniele or speck.

PARMA HAM, ROCKET AND BUBBLING BLUE CHEESE

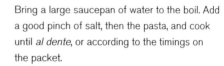

300 g dried pasta, such as pappardelle or lasagnette

2 tablespoons olive oil

8 slices Parma ham

250 g cherry tomatoes

2 Bresse Blue or mini Cambazola cheeses, 150 g each

2 tablespoons Marsala or sherry

2 tablespoons chopped fresh flat leaf parsley

a handful of rocket

salt and freshly ground black pepper

Serves 4

Bring a large saucepan of water to the boil. Add a good pinch of salt, then the pasta, and cook until *al dente*, or according to the timings on the packet.

Meanwhile, heat a little of the oil in a non-stick frying pan, add the Parma ham and cook for 1 minute on each side until crisp. Remove and drain on kitchen paper. Add the remaining oil to the pan. When hot, add the cherry tomatoes and cook for 3–4 minutes until split and softened.

Meanwhile, cut each cheese in half crossways, put cut side up under an overhead grill and cook for 2–3 minutes, until golden and bubbling.

Break the Parma ham into pieces and add to the tomato pan. Add the Marsala or sherry, parsley and salt and pepper to taste.

Drain the pasta well and return it to the warm pan. Add the Parma ham and tomato mixture and toss gently to mix. Divide between 4 bowls or plates and sprinkle with rocket. Using a spatula, slide a bubbling cheese half on top of each. Sprinkle with black pepper and serve.

WHITE SPAGHETTI

This is one of those storecupboard dishes that saves your life when you get home late, tired and hungry. Keep a stock of anchovies, olive oil and spaghetti in the cupboard and you can always make this at short notice.

150 g dried pasta, such as spaghetti

6 tablespoons olive oil

4 garlic cloves, halved

6 anchovy fillets in oil, drained

salt and freshly ground black pepper

Serves 2

Bring a large saucepan of water to the boil. Add a good pinch of salt, then the pasta, and cook until *al dente*, or according to the timings on the packet.

Put the olive oil and garlic into a small saucepan and heat very gently over low heat for 4–5 minutes until the garlic is pale golden but not browned. Remove and discard the garlic.

Add the anchovies and 100 ml water to the pan and simmer rapidly, whisking with the fork until the anchovies have almost dissolved into the mixture. Add plenty of black pepper and a tiny pinch of salt.

Drain the pasta and return it to the warm pan. Add the anchovy mixture and toss well to mix. Divide between 2 bowls or plates and serve.

MUSSELS IN WHITE WINE WITH LINGUINE

A delicious, low fat pasta dish? Yes it's true. Better still, it's ready to serve in 15 minutes.

300 g dried pasta, such as linguine or tagliatelle

150 ml dry white wine

2 garlic cloves, finely chopped

1 red chilli, deseeded and finely chopped

1 kg fresh mussels in shells

2 tablespoons chopped fresh flat leaf parsley

salt and freshly ground black pepper

olive oil, to serve

Serves 4

Bring a large saucepan of water to the boil. Add a good pinch of salt, then the pasta, and cook until *al dente*, or according to the timings on the packet.

Meanwhile, put the wine, garlic and chilli into another large saucepan, bring to the boil and simmer rapidly for 5 minutes. Add the mussels, cover with a lid and cook for 5 minutes, shaking the pan from time to time until all the shells have opened. Discard any that remain closed.

Drain the pasta and return it to the warm pan. Add the parsley and the mussels and toss gently to mix. Divide between 4 bowls, sprinkle with olive oil, then serve.

A lovely, summery dish to make the most of fragrant garden herbs. I serve the prawns on skewers to add a sense of occasion (and to make them easier to turn while cooking), but you can always cook them loose and add to the pasta just before serving.

HERBED TAGLIATELLE WITH PRAWN SKEWERS

350 g dried pasta, such as tagliatelle, linguine or fettuccine

20 uncooked tiger prawns, peeled with tails on

2 garlic cloves, crushed

½ teaspoon crushed dried chillies

4 tablespoons olive oil

1 teaspoon chopped fresh rosemary

2 tablespoons chopped fresh flat leaf parsley

1 tablespoon snipped fresh chives

a handful of rocket

salt and freshly ground black pepper

1 lemon, cut into wedges, to serve

4 wooden skewers, soaked in water for 30 minutes

Serves 4

Bring a large saucepan of water to the boil. Add a pinch of salt, then the pasta, and cook until *al dente,* or according to the timings on the packet.

Meanwhile, put the prawns into a bowl and add the garlic, dried chillies, 1 tablespoon of the olive oil, and salt and pepper to taste. Mix well, then thread 5 prawns onto each skewer.

Preheat a stove-top grill pan until hot. Add the prawn skewers to the hot pan and cook for 3 minutes on each side until pink and cooked through. Remove and keep them warm. Add the lemon wedges to the pan and cook quickly for 30 seconds on each side.

Drain the pasta and return it to the warm pan. Add the remaining oil, rosemary, parsley, chives and rocket, with salt and pepper to taste. Toss gently, then divide between 4 serving bowls. Top each with a prawn skewer and a lemon wedge for squeezing, then serve.

CREAMY SMOKED SALMON SAUCE

Smoked salmon adds a lovely delicate flavour to this
dish. Add it right at the last moment so it doesn't
overcook or break into tiny pieces.

**300 g dried pasta, such as
fusilli bucati or farfalle**

300 ml double cream

2 garlic cloves, crushed

**200 g smoked salmon,
cut into 1 cm strips**

**4 tablespoons freshly grated
Parmesan cheese, plus
extra to serve**

**salt and freshly ground
black pepper**

**2 tablespoons snipped fresh
chives, to serve**

Serves 4

Bring a large saucepan of water
to the boil. Add a pinch of salt, then
the pasta, and cook until *al dente,*
or according to the timings on
the packet.

Meanwhile, put the cream and garlic
into a small saucepan. Add salt and
pepper to taste and heat gently until
warmed through.

Drain the pasta and return it to the
warm pan. Add the cream, smoked
salmon and Parmesan, toss gently,
then divide between 4 bowls or
plates. Sprinkle with chives and
extra Parmesan and serve.

This is the speciality of my friend and colleague, Jenny, who can rustle it up in a matter of minutes. All you need is fresh broccoli and a few basic ingredients.

BROCCOLI AND PINE NUT PESTO

175 g dried pasta, such as penne or fusilli

175 g broccoli, cut into florets

2 tablespoons pine nuts

3 tablespoons olive oil

3 garlic cloves, finely chopped

1 red chilli, deseeded and finely chopped

½ lemon

fresh shavings of Parmesan cheese, to serve

salt and freshly ground black pepper

Serves 2

Bring a large saucepan of water to the boil. Add a good pinch of salt, then the pasta, and cook until *al dente,* or according to the timings on the packet.

Cook the broccoli in a separate saucepan of boiling, salted water for 10–12 minutes until very soft. Meanwhile, heat a dry frying pan until hot, add the pine nuts and cook, turning them frequently, until golden and toasted. Transfer to a plate and set aside.

Heat the olive oil in a small saucepan and add the garlic and chilli. Gently cook for 2–3 minutes until softened. Remove from the heat and set aside.

Drain the broccoli, return it to the pan and mash coarsely with a fork.

Drain the pasta and return it to the warm pan. Add the mashed broccoli, garlic and chilli oil and toasted pine nuts. Mix well, squeeze in a little lemon juice and add salt and pepper to taste.

Divide between 2 serving bowls and top with fresh Parmesan shavings. Sprinkle with pepper and serve.

vegetables
and herbs

ROASTED AUBERGINE AND TOMATO

Angela, another friend and colleague, adores aubergines and puts them in just about everything she cooks – this is her recipe.

2 aubergines, cut into 3 cm cubes

500 g ripe tomatoes, quartered

2 garlic cloves, halved

4 tablespoons olive oil

300 g dried pasta, such as fusilli or fusilli bucati

1 shallot, finely chopped

2 tablespoons chopped fresh mint

2 tablespoons chopped fresh coriander

juice of 1 lime

salt and freshly ground black pepper

Serves 4

Put the aubergine, tomatoes and garlic into a large roasting tin. Add 2 tablespoons of the olive oil and mix. Sprinkle with salt and pepper and cook in a preheated oven at 200°C (400°F) Gas 6 for 30–40 minutes, turning the vegetables from time to time, until the aubergine is tender and golden.

Meanwhile, bring a large saucepan of water to the boil. Add a good pinch of salt, then the pasta, and cook until *al dente,* or according to the timings on the packet.

Drain the pasta well and return it to the warm pan. Add the roasted aubergine and tomatoes, then the shallot, mint, coriander and lime juice. Add the remaining oil and toss well to mix. Divide between 4 bowls or plates and serve.

FUSILLI WITH SALSA VERDE AND CHAR-GRILLED CHEESE

My salsa verde varies each time I make it, according to the herbs I have to hand – parsley should always be the base, but feel free to add basil, tarragon or mint instead of the coriander. The cheese is an added extra and not essential.

300 g dried pasta, such as fusilli

250 g halloumi or provolone cheese, cut into 1 cm thick slices

2 tablespoons plain flour

1 teaspoon cracked black pepper

Salsa Verde

2 anchovy fillets in oil, drained

1 tablespoon salted capers, rinsed well

1 green chilli, deseeded and finely chopped

1 garlic clove, crushed

3 tablespoons chopped fresh flat leaf parsley

1 tablespoon chopped fresh coriander

2 teaspoons Dijon mustard

4 tablespoons olive oil

1 tablespoon white wine vinegar

 Serves 4

Bring a large saucepan of water to the boil. Add a good pinch of salt, then the pasta, and cook until *al dente,* or according to the timings on the packet.

Meanwhile, to make the Salsa Verde, put the anchovy fillets and capers onto a chopping board and, using a heavy knife, chop finely. Put the chilli and garlic on top and chop again until very finely chopped. Transfer to a bowl and add the herbs, mustard, 3 tablespoons of the oil and the vinegar.

Heat the remaining oil in a stove-top grill pan until hot. Put the flour onto a small plate, add the black pepper and mix. Dip each cheese slice in the flour to coat on both sides, shaking off any excess. Cook in the grill pan for 1–2 minutes on each side until golden brown, then remove and drain on kitchen paper.

Drain the pasta well and return it to the warm pan. Add the Salsa Verde and toss to mix. Divide between 4 bowls or plates, arrange the cheese on top, then serve.

Tantalizing pockets of melting garlic butter flavoured with herbs and cheese complement the succulent chunks of roast pumpkin. The flavoured butter is also brilliant for making garlic bread – it melts between the slices of bread to a deliciously moist and stretchy filling.

SAGE, LEMON AND MOZZARELLA BUTTER WITH ROASTED PUMPKIN

2 tablespoons olive oil

500 g pumpkin or butternut squash

1 teaspoon cumin seeds

150 g mozzarella cheese, drained and coarsely chopped

50 g butter, softened

2 garlic cloves, crushed

2 teaspoons chopped fresh sage leaves, plus extra whole leaves, to serve

grated zest and juice of 1 lemon

300 g dried pasta, such as fusilli bucati or cavatappi

salt and freshly ground black pepper

greaseproof paper

Serves 4

Put the olive oil into a roasting tin and transfer to a preheated oven at 200°C (400F°) Gas 6 for 5 minutes, until hot.

Using a small, sharp knife, peel the pumpkin or butternut, remove the seeds and cut the flesh into cubes, about 2.5 cm.

Add the cumin seeds to the hot oil in the roasting tin, then add the pumpkin or butternut and salt and pepper to taste. Toss to coat. Roast in the oven for 30 minutes, turning the pumpkin or butternut from time to time until tender and golden brown.

Put the mozzarella, butter, garlic, sage, lemon zest and juice, salt and pepper into a food processor. Blend to a coarse paste. Transfer to a sheet of greaseproof paper and roll into a cylinder. Chill for at least 20 minutes or until firm enough to slice.

Meanwhile, bring a large saucepan of water to the boil. Add a good pinch of salt, then the pasta, and cook until *al dente*, or according to the timings on the packet.

Drain the pasta and return it to the warm pan. Add the roasted pumpkin or butternut. Slice or dice the mozzarella butter and add to the pasta. Toss, divide between 4 bowls or plates, top with sage leaves and serve.

soups

PASTA E FAGIOLI

This hearty soup of pasta and beans is a classic from the region of Puglia in Italy – the pasta shapes traditionally used are orecchiette, meaning 'little ears'.

2 tablespoons olive oil

1 small onion, finely chopped

2 garlic cloves, finely chopped

1 potato, diced

2 ripe tomatoes, coarsely chopped

1.25 litres chicken or vegetable stock

a sprig of thyme, sage or rosemary

800 g canned cannellini beans, drained

150 g small dried pasta shapes, such as orecchiette

a pinch of crushed dried chillies

salt and freshly ground black pepper

freshly grated Parmesan cheese, to serve

Serves 4

Heat the oil in a large saucepan, add the onion, garlic and potato and cook for 3–4 minutes until golden. Add the tomatoes and cook for 2–3 minutes until softened.

Add the stock, herbs, beans, pasta, dried chillies, salt and pepper. Bring to the boil, then simmer for about 10 minutes, until the pasta and potatoes are cooked.

Ladle into 4 bowls and serve sprinkled with a little Parmesan.

A very light, fragrant version of a soup that can sometimes be rather heavy. It has added sparkle thanks to the last-minute addition of fresh pesto.

SUMMER MINESTRONE

50 g small dried pasta shapes, such as anellini or fedelini

1 tablespoon olive oil

1 red onion, chopped

1 garlic clove, finely chopped

2 celery stalks, thinly sliced

150 g baby carrots, thinly sliced

2 plum tomatoes, coarsely chopped

1.25 litres vegetable stock

150 g runner beans, thinly sliced

2 tablespoons Classic Basil Pesto (page 13)

salt and freshly ground black pepper

1 tablespoon freshly grated Parmesan cheese, to serve

Serves 4

Bring a large saucepan of water to the boil. Add a good pinch of salt, then the pasta, and cook until *al dente*, or according to the timings on the packet. Drain well.

Meanwhile, heat the oil in another large saucepan, add the onion and garlic and cook gently for 3 minutes. Add the celery and carrots and cook for a further 2 minutes. Add the tomatoes and cook for 2 minutes.

Add the stock and beans, bring to the boil, then simmer for 5–10 minutes, until the vegetables are cooked and tender.

Add the drained pasta, stir in the pesto and add salt and pepper to taste. Divide between 4 bowls, sprinkle with Parmesan and serve.

CONCHIGLIETTE SOUP WITH PEAS, ARTICHOKES AND CHILLI

An incredibly speedy soup that has a wonderful, fresh flavour, yet is made almost entirely from storecupboard ingredients. Enjoy a taste of summer all year round.

1 tablespoon olive oil

1 onion, finely chopped

2 garlic cloves, finely chopped

2 red chillies, thinly sliced into rings

4 slices smoked streaky bacon, finely chopped

1 teaspoon fresh marjoram or oregano

400 g canned artichoke hearts in water, drained and quartered

100 g frozen peas

1.25 litres chicken stock

75 g dried pasta shapes, such as conchigliette or gnocchetti

salt and freshly ground black pepper

2 tablespoons freshly grated Parmesan cheese, to serve

Serves 4

Heat the oil in a large saucepan, add the onion, garlic, chilli and bacon and cook for 4–5 minutes until golden.

Add the marjoram or oregano, artichokes and peas and stir-fry for 2 minutes. Add the stock, bring to the boil, then simmer for 10 minutes.

Meanwhile, bring another large saucepan of water to the boil. Add a good pinch of salt, then the pasta, and cook until *al dente*, or according to the timings on the packet.

Drain the pasta and add it to the soup. Divide between 4 bowls, sprinkle with Parmesan, then serve.

baked pasta

CLASSIC LASAGNE

It's easy to buy lasagne that requires no precooking, but I find it draws moisture from the sauce as it cooks, and the finished dish can be dry. I prefer the little extra effort of boiling the lasagne first.

500 g dried lasagne

1 quantity Bolognese Sauce (page 15)

300 g mozzarella cheese, drained and diced

4 tablespoons freshly grated Parmesan cheese

salt and freshly ground black pepper

White Sauce

1 litre milk

1 small garlic clove

50 g butter

50 g plain flour

a baking dish, about 30 x 20 x 7 cm

Serves 8

Bring a large saucepan of water to the boil. Add a pinch of salt, then the lasagne sheets, one at a time so that they don't stick together. Cook for 5 minutes, then drain and tip the lasagne into a bowl of cold water. Drain again and pat dry with kitchen paper.

To make the White Sauce, put the milk and garlic into a small saucepan and heat gently until warm. Melt the butter in a separate saucepan, then stir in the flour and cook for 1 minute. Gradually add the warm milk, stirring constantly to make a smooth sauce. Bring to the boil, then simmer for 2–3 minutes. Remove and discard the garlic clove. Add salt and pepper to taste.

Put 3–4 tablespoons of the Bolognese Sauce into the baking dish, spread evenly across the base of the dish and cover with a layer of lasagne. Spoon over some White Sauce and a few pieces of mozzarella and continue adding layers, starting with another layer of Bolognese Sauce and finishing with the White Sauce and mozzarella, until all the ingredients have been used. Sprinkle with freshly ground black pepper and Parmesan, then bake in a preheated oven at 190°C (375°F) Gas 5 for 30 minutes until the top is crusty and golden.

OVEN-ROASTED SPICY MACARONI

Inspired by paella, the Spanish rice dish, this is absolutely delicious, and never fails to impress and delight. It's all cooked in the oven, so really couldn't be easier.

250 g cherry tomatoes

1 red onion, finely chopped

2 garlic cloves, finely chopped

2 tablespoons olive oil

300 g small macaroni

4 boneless, skinless chicken thighs, quartered crossways

200 g chorizo sausage, thickly sliced

2 teaspoons chopped fresh rosemary

1 litre chicken stock

a pinch of saffron threads

8 large, uncooked prawns

salt and freshly ground black pepper

a handful of basil leaves, torn, to serve

a heavy roasting tin

Serves 4

Put the cherry tomatoes into the roasting tin and sprinkle with the red onion, garlic and olive oil. Roast in a preheated oven at 220°C (400°F) Gas 7 for 20 minutes until the tomatoes are soft.

Remove from the oven and add the macaroni, chicken, chorizo, rosemary, stock, saffron, salt and pepper. Mix well and return it to the oven to bake for 30 minutes.

Add the prawns and bake for a further 5 minutes until the pasta and chicken are cooked. Sprinkle with basil and serve.

600 ml tomato passata

150 ml red wine

1 teaspoon brown sugar

1 garlic clove, crushed

1 bay leaf

1 tablespoon olive oil

12 dried cannelloni tubes

Parsley and Pancetta Filling

2 tablespoons olive oil

1 onion, finely chopped

2 garlic cloves, finely chopped

125 g cubed pancetta

4 tablespoons chopped
fresh flat leaf parsley

200 g fresh
white breadcrumbs

150 ml double cream

grated zest and juice of 1 lemon

150 g mozzarella cheese,
drained and cubed

salt and freshly
ground black pepper

a baking dish, about 30 x 20 cm

Serves 4

PARSLEY AND PANCETTA CANNELLONI

I don't precook the cannelloni tubes, as it makes them difficult to stuff. So to compensate for the moisture they will absorb as they cook, the sauce should be runny – it will become thickened and rich.

Put the passata, wine, sugar, garlic, bay leaf and olive oil into a saucepan. Add salt and pepper to taste and bring to the boil. Cover with a lid and simmer for 15 minutes.

To make the filling, heat 1 tablespoon of the oil in a saucepan, add the onion, garlic and pancetta and cook for 4–5 minutes until softened and golden. Add the parsley, breadcrumbs, cream, lemon zest and juice and salt and pepper to taste.

Spoon the filling mixture into the cannelloni tubes and arrange the stuffed tubes in the baking dish. Pour the tomato sauce over the top and sprinkle with the mozzarella. Bake in a preheated oven at 190°C (375°F) Gas 5 for 40 minutes, or until the top is bubbling and golden and the pasta is cooked through.

A simplified version of that old-time favourite, macaroni cheese, but with no flour and no risk of lumps.

THREE CHEESE BAKED PENNE

350 g dried pasta, such as penne

400 g mascarpone cheese

2 tablespoons wholegrain mustard

300 g Fontina cheese, grated

4 tablespoons freshly grated Parmesan cheese

salt and freshly ground black pepper

a baking dish, about 30 x 20 cm

Serves 4

Bring a large saucepan of water to the boil. Add a good pinch of salt, then the pasta, and cook until *al dente*, or according to the timings on the packet.

Drain the pasta well and return it to the warm pan. Add the mascarpone and stir to mix. Add the mustard, Fontina and Parmesan, with salt and pepper to taste. Stir to mix.

Transfer to the baking dish and cook in a preheated oven at 200°C (400°F) Gas 6 for 25–30 minutes until golden and bubbling.

filled pasta

PORK AND PARMESAN RAVIOLI

Pork and cheese are not a common pairing, but
they make a good match if full-bodied flavours
such as garlic and sun-dried tomatoes are included
in the mix. The filling can be made in advance and
kept covered and refrigerated for up to a day.

1 garlic clove, chopped

**1 red chilli, deseeded
and finely chopped**

**4 sun-dried tomatoes in oil,
drained and coarsely chopped**

500 g pork mince

1 teaspoon fresh thyme leaves

**4 tablespoons freshly grated
Parmesan cheese, plus
extra to serve**

**1 quantity Fresh Pasta Dough,
rolled (page 11)**

**1 quantity Tomato with
Double Basil sauce (page 12),
warmed**

a handful of basil leaves, to serve

**salt and freshly
ground black pepper**

Serves 4

Put the garlic, chilli and sun-dried tomatoes into a food
processor and process until finely chopped. Add the pork,
thyme, Parmesan, salt and pepper, then process again until
evenly blended.

Put a sheet of rolled pasta onto a lightly floured surface. Put
tablespoons of the mixture in evenly-spaced mounds on the
dough, leaving about 4 cm between each mound. Cover with a
second sheet of rolled pasta dough and, using your fingers,
press firmly round the mounds to seal, excluding any air.

Using a knife, cut lines between the mounds to make separate
squares, about 8 cm each. Repeat with the remaining pasta and
filling to make 20 ravioli squares in total.

Bring a large saucepan of water to the boil. Add a good pinch
of salt, then the ravioli, and cook for 3–4 minutes until they rise
to the surface and are cooked through. Drain carefully and
return to the warm pan. Add the warm tomato sauce and stir to
coat. Divide between 4 bowls or plates, sprinkle with basil, black
pepper and Parmesan, then serve.

CRAB TORTELLINI

Make these very small shapes in batches, rolling out one sheet of dough at a time, so that the pasta doesn't dry out as you are working.

2 tablespoons olive oil

1 shallot, finely chopped

2 garlic cloves, finely chopped

1 red chilli, deseeded and finely chopped

1 tablespoon chopped fresh tarragon, plus extra leaves to serve

grated zest and juice of 1 lemon

250 g fresh or canned white crabmeat, drained if canned

1 quantity Fresh Pasta Dough (page 11)

50 g unsalted butter, cubed

salt and freshly ground black pepper

a plain pastry cutter, 5 cm diameter

Serves 4

Heat the oil in a small frying pan, add the shallot, garlic and chilli and cook for 4–5 minutes until softened and golden. Remove from the heat and stir in the tarragon, half the lemon zest, the crabmeat, salt and black pepper.

Divide the pasta dough into 6 and roll out 1 piece (see page 11). Put the sheet of rolled dough onto a lightly floured surface and, using the pastry cutter, stamp out 10–12 rounds. Put a small teaspoon of the mixture in the centre of each circle, brush water lightly round the edge of the circle and fold over to enclose the filling. Seal, excluding as much air as possible. Bring the two tips together and pinch firmly to seal them. Working in batches, repeat with the remaining pasta dough and filling mixture.

Bring a large saucepan of water to the boil. Add a good pinch of salt, then the tortellini, and cook for 3–4 minutes until they rise to the surface and are cooked through.

Meanwhile, put the remaining lemon zest and juice into a small saucepan over low heat. Add the butter, 1 or 2 cubes at a time, stirring with a whisk until smooth and foaming. Carefully drain the tortellini, return them to the warm pan and add the lemon butter. Stir briefly, then divide between 4 bowls or plates. Top with a few tarragon leaves and plenty of black pepper, then serve.

Note If you are not cooking the tortellini immediately, arrange in a single layer on a tray lined with greaseproof paper, cover with another sheet of greaseproof paper and chill for up to 2 hours.

Taleggio is a soft cheese and not easy to slice thinly. A good trick is to put the cheese in the freezer for 10–15 minutes before slicing. Truffle oil has an earthy, intense flavour that goes beautifully with mushrooms – add a splash to the cooked mezzalune.

MUSHROOM MEZZALUNE

2 tablespoons olive oil, plus extra to serve

1 garlic clove, finely chopped

250 g small chestnut or field mushrooms, sliced

2 tablespoons Marsala or medium sherry

1 quantity Fresh Pasta Dough, rolled (page 11)

200 g Taleggio cheese, thinly sliced

6 slices Parma ham, halved

salt and freshly ground black pepper

to serve

olive or truffle oil

basil leaves

a round bowl, about 14 cm diameter

Serves 4

Heat the oil in a frying pan, add the garlic and cook for 1 minute. Add the mushrooms and salt and pepper to taste and cook for 3–4 minutes until golden. Add the Marsala or sherry, remove from the heat and let cool.

Put a rolled pasta sheet onto a lightly floured surface. Put the bowl, upside down, on top of the pasta and cut round it with a knife. Repeat to make 12 rounds. Put a slice of Taleggio on one side of each round, spoon over the mushrooms and top with a piece of Parma ham, folded to fit if necessary. Dampen the edges lightly with water and fold each circle over to form a semi-circle, pressing the edges together firmly to enclose the filling and seal.

Bring a large saucepan of water to the boil. Add a good pinch of salt, then half the mezzalune. Cook for 3–4 minutes until they rise to the surface and are cooked through. Drain carefully and keep them warm while you cook the remaining mezzalune. Divide between 4 bowls or plates, sprinkle with olive or truffle oil and basil leaves, then serve.

Note For making ahead and storing, see the tortellini note on page 60.

index